the return of the tree people

the return of the tree people

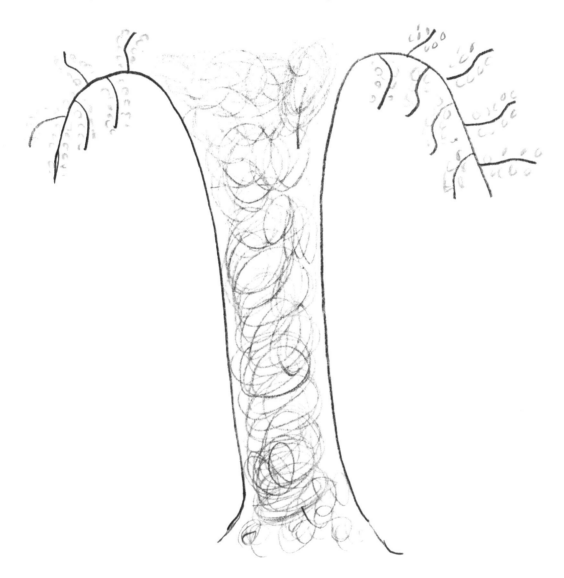

an artistic, musical adventure

by Stephen Cohen, Rich Hinrichsen, and Julie Keefe

The Return of The Tree People:
an Artistic, Musical Adventure
by Stephen Cohen, Rich Hinrichsen, and Julie Keefe

Music Credits:
"Canzone di un Cuore Triste" (pages 22 and 23) © 1978 Richard A. Hinrichsen
"I Hit Song" (page 26) © 2012 Stephen Cohen
"Tale for 2" (page 27) © 2022 Rich Hinrichsen and Stephen Cohen
"Mad Waltz" (page 28) © 2011 Stephen Cohen and Rich Hinrichsen
"Walking Willow Tree" (page 32) © 2012 Stephen Cohen
"Lullaby" (pages 36 and 37) 2006 Stephen Cohen

Printed in the United States of America

First Edition: May 2022
ISBN 978-1-946970-11-4
Library of Congress Control Number: 2022908443

Published by

Wake-Robin Press
An imprint of redbat books
La Grande, OR 97850
www.wakerobinpress.com

Text set in Chaparral Pro, Chelsea Market Open, and Felt Tip Woman

Cover Art drawn by
Stephen Cohen

Cover Design & Book Layout by
redbat design | www.redbatdesign.com

table of contents

we dedicate this book

to all the trees around us—the lives of these trees
help make our lives on this earth possible

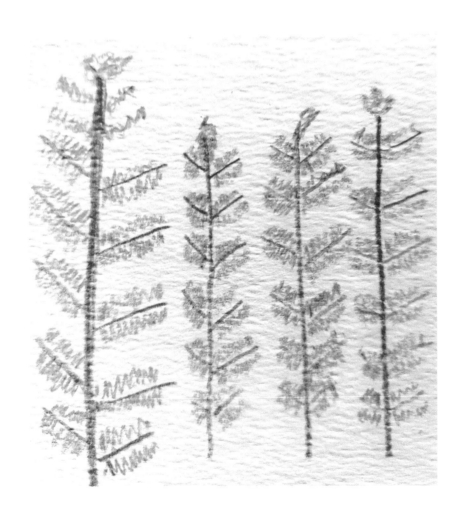

the beginning and the return

the tree people

The Beginning of The Tree People:

The Tree People was recorded in 1979 at Rockin' A Ranch, a studio in the woods near Eugene, Oregon in one weekend, with musicians Stephen Cohen, Jeff Stier, Rachel Laderman and James Thornbury. 1,000 vinyl records were pressed, and the album was released locally. Stephen and Jeff recorded a second Tree People album, *Human Voices*, and released it as a cassette in 1984.

(drawings for both albums by Stephen Cohen)

The Tree People in the new century:

Record collectors around the globe somehow discovered *The Tree People* in this century, leading to record companies in Japan and Spain reissuing it, to international acclaim. *Human Voices* was reissued by Guerssen Records of Spain. Guerssen Records released a third record album in 2010, *It's My Story*, recorded with Stephen, Jeff, and a new member of the band, double bassist Rich Hinrichsen.

(photo by Chris Leck, graphics by Redbat Design)

The Return of The Tree People:

The Return of The Tree People was recorded in 2021 at Dead Aunt Thelma's Studio in Portland, Oregon in one weekend, with musicians Stephen Cohen, Rich Hinrichsen, Maeve Stier (daughter of the late Jeff Stier), John Savage, Jen Harrison and Ron Tuttle. The album and this book were released in 2022.

(drawing by Stephen Cohen)

above: Rich, Jeff and Stephen at Dead Aunt Thelma's Studio, 2009. (photo by Ben Sussman)

below: Rich, Stephen and Maeve at Dead Aunt Thelma's Studio, 2021. (photo by Julie Keefe)

Stephen and Jeff, Eugene, Oregon, 1984.

the return of the tree people

a musician, a flute player...

...world class recorder player, a percussionist, a husband, a friend, partner, a gourmet chef, a bicycle rider, and father, Jeff brought inspiration and magic to the world. Jeff had a poetic, charismatic insight that he brought to everything he did, especially when he performed with The Tree People, where his improvisational genius could weave transcendent, fluent melodies. He listened to classical music constantly and was so proud of his daughter Maeve when she chose to pursue a Bachelors in classical voice at Portland State University. He was so happy to hear her perform leading roles with Portland State Opera and to sing with the Oregon Symphony.

—Jennifer Johnston

Maeve and Stephen, Portland, Oregon, 2022. (photo by Brian Bauer)

legends of the tree people

—lyrics by Stephen Cohen and Jeff Stier

Be advised The Tree People are a gentle folk who inhabit woodlands and other arboreal landscapes. Legend has it, when winter approached, The Tree People entered a giant tree, through a secret passageway, where they found shelter from the elements. They passed the winter telling stories and filling the forest with muted echoes of music.

Retiring for the night, The Tree People placed their faces in intricately carved wooden boxes. Then they walked down the pathways of sleep and dreamed strange and ineffable dreams. In the morning they opened a box at random and took a new face for the day. Where one had been handsome, he now might be homely, where one had a crooked nose, now her nose might be perfectly formed. This invariably caused gales of laughter.

And when spring arrived, the band of Tree People musicians, magicians, mathematicians, politicians, technicians, inventors, dissenters, presenters, thinkers, tinkers and tradespeople began their long procession to the sea, where they lay their wooden bodies in the water and let the waves carry them to distant lands.

when rich joined...

...The Tree People in late 2007, Jeff sent him some poetic thoughts about The Tree People:

> *Be advised that The Tree People are a gentle folk who inhabit woodlands and other arboreal landscapes. The branches of many of the trees in these places are adorned with musical instruments of various sorts. It is not clear whether the instruments play themselves—perhaps when the wind blows.*
> (Jeff Stier, November 2007)

Album reviews of the reissued 1st album called The Tree People "the legendary Tree People," "psych folk pioneers" and "fathers of freak folk." Rich responded, "A lot of my feeling about The Tree People is contained in my words to Jeff. I wrote these as a response to learning that The Tree People were legendary...."

> *The Tree People are legendary. You are the bird singing in a tree, and I a moose calling for a mate. The Tree People are legendary. Stephen coaxes sweet chords, while dodging one, two, three, and four with voice. The Tree People are legendary. The gods dance and nod. The Tree People are legendary. The drums ground melody with tribal beat. The primeval human delights. The butterfly smiles.* (Rich Hinrichsen, 2007)

With The Tree People I have a lot of room to experiment with melodies and play non-traditional things on the bass instead of roots and fifths. I'm not there just to hold a beat. With the way Stephen plays guitar, it's more like chamber music than folk music. He's playing intricate melodies while playing bass notes and chords—an orchestra of six strings. (Rich Hinrichsen, 2022)

my good, good friend

—Stephen Cohen

Hello my good, good friend, it's so good to see you again

Yes, we did walk in the hot sun and the pouring rain

Happy and sad, good and bad

So much joy, too much pain

Goodbye my good, good friend

movie lot

—Stephen Cohen

They line up every morning at the movie lot, just to see the famous

I'd rather have your autograph

They live inside the movie screens, inside the trade magazines

You can do anything the rich can do, you can show the famous a thing or two

You've been places they've never been, you've done things they've never seen

You can do anything they can do

They line up every evening at a choice venue, just to see the famous

I'd rather look at you

They live inside the movie screens, inside the trade magazines

You can do anything the rich can do, you can show the famous a thing or two

You've been places they've never been, you've done things they've never seen

You can do anything they can do

They watch the late-night outtake interview, just to hear the famous

I'd rather hear from you

We live outside the movie screens, outside the trade magazines

You can do anything the rich can do, you can show the famous a thing or two

You've been places they've never been, you've done things they've never seen

You can do anything they can do

You can do anything they can do, better

the musicians

clockwise from top left:
John on saxophone at Dead Aunt Thelma's, Maeve at Dead Aunt Thelma's, Rich and Stephen at the Old Church Concert Hall, Rich with double bass at the Old Church Concert Hall, Ron playing drums at Dead Aunt Thelma's, Stephen on guitar and Jen on horn at the Old Church Concert Hall.

"Every song, every take was a grouping of musical snapshots that told a story. There were never more than three takes, and many times just one. Each take had its own thing to say."

—Dean Baskerville

left: Stephen's homemade 1-string thing instrument

above and page 15: John playing the saxophone (with Maeve seen in the background) and Stephen playing panpipes as well as harmonica at Dead Aunt Thelma's Studio. (photos by Julie Keefe)

hearing test

"I'd played with Stephen before for a children's concert and enjoyed his freewheelin' whimsy, so I anticipated a recording session with The Tree People that would live up to the freak/psyche-folk descriptors I'd read about. When it came time to record 'Hearing Test,' I had a couple moments of sheer joy. First, there was Stephen's beginning of the song with his self-made 1-string-thing and harmonica that set the tone for this playpen of the ears. I had an uncontrollable wide-mouthed-grin of delight as the rest of the band came rollicking in. Then, I look through the window of the sound booth to see vocalist and accordionist Maeve Stier preparing to play her kazoo—an angled horn recalling that of Dizzy's bent trumpet, and its ensuing sound resembling a humming, giant plastic bee."

—John Savage

mathematics

—Stephen Cohen

we have to talk about the mathematics

so much depends on the mathematics

and begins and ends with the mathematics

let's talk about the numbers

this is about the mathematics

I don't have to shout about the mathematics

we can figure out the mathematics

let's talk about the numbers

we have to talk about the mathematics

so much depends on the mathematics

and begins and ends with the mathematics

let's talk about the numbers

this is about the mathematics

we can figure out the mathematics

and factor in the mathematics

let's talk about the numbers

Rich is both an accomplished mathematician and musician, which no doubt influenced Stephen's song "Mathematics."

· · ·

$$\hat{B} = SA^k WS^T (SWS^T)^{-1}$$

"This equation allows one to reduce the number of age categories used when making population projections. It is the subject of a paper I will soon submit to the journal *Demographic Research*. I apply it to populations in 42 different European countries. The equation can also be used to reduce the number of size categories when projecting numbers of trees in a forest."

—Rich Hinrichsen, 2022

play us

"Play Us" is a musical exercise that is fun to do live in the studio. Stephen plays three notes on his 3-string *Play Me* sculpture, then pauses and points to each musician in turn, who plays a note in the space, plays another note in the next space, and then another. After everyone has a turn, the piece ends with everyone playing an extended note at once, followed by the distant ringing of a bronze gong.

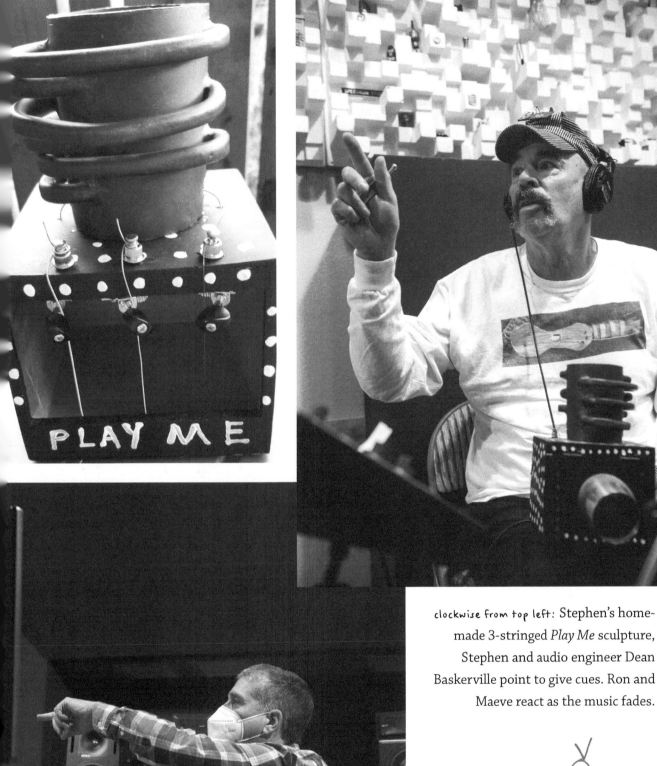

clockwise from top left: Stephen's home-made 3-stringed *Play Me* sculpture, Stephen and audio engineer Dean Baskerville point to give cues. Ron and Maeve react as the music fades.

page 20: "Ally the Cat" painting by Alexa Wiley.

the return of the tree people

ally the cat

—Stephen Cohen

A green-eyed gray kitten was found in an alley by a woman named Ally

That kitten came to live with me, and took the name of Ally

above left: Stephen plays cigar box guitar on "Ally the Cat." above right: Stephen plays his one-of-a-kind, custom-made miniature guitar and is joined by Maeve's layered clapping and Rich's tapping on Miniature Sliding.

canzone di un cuore triste

—Rich Hinrichsen

canzone

"High school meant leaving the logging town where I was born to live in Shadow Wood condominiums in Lynnwood, Washington after my Mom divorced. High school meant walking to school in the dark to catch a bus to the only high school with an orchestra in the school district. High school meant learning to play piano on the Cable-Nelson baby grand my Mom bought with the money she earned selling 100s of purses she sewed by hand. High school meant falling in love with two sisters who lived across the street. It meant sitting at the piano to write a sad song to help a bewildered teenager feel better."

—Rich Hinrichsen

top: Rich plays piano, 1977. bottom: Rich in Italy.

1 hit song

—Stephen Cohen

If I had just one hit song,

    I would not be just another one hit wonder

If I had just one hit song,

    everyone could tag along, if I had just one hit song

If I had just one hit song,

    I would not be a one hit man, not a flash in the pan

If I had just one hit song,

    everyone would sing along, if I had just one hit song

tale for 2

—Rich Hinrichsen and Stephen Cohen

Double Bass

mad waltz

—Stephen Cohen and Rich Hinrichsen

the return of the tree people

DATE

SUBJECT   TECHNICAL DATA

above: The Tree People at the
Hult Center in Eugene, 1984.

left: Jeff plays flute at the
White Eagle in Portland, 2007.
(photo by Chris Leck)

above: "Log Hoist Ruins." (photo by Stephen Cohen)

the return of the tree people

ruins

—Stephen Cohen

no, it's not the first time, it won't be the last

that something has come and something has passed

into ruin

people through the ages, hear my call

it seems that we always must fall

into ruin

and if you're still left, when so much has gone

there's nothing left but to live on

rise from the ruins

but the spirit still lingers like voices in the hills

in the conversations of the people who still

rise from the ruins, glide through the ruins, slide through the ruins

walking willow tree

—Stephen Cohen

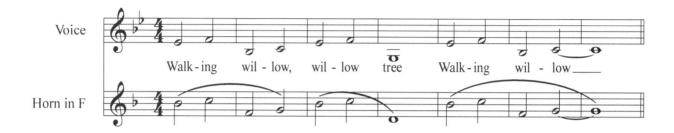

walking willow, walking willow, walking willow tree

I knew you before, but I just didn't see,
    just how much you would come to mean to me

now every day, you and me, sit and talk under the walking willow tree

walking willow, walking willow, walking willow tree

I wrote this melody when I was just fifteen, dreaming under
    the walking willow tree

now time has passed, and you and me, sit and laugh under
    the walking willow tree

walking willow, walking willow, walking willow tree

there's no place else I'd rather be, sitting under the walking willow tree

now every day, you and me, sit and talk under the walking willow tree

walking willow, walking willow, walking willow tree

the tree people in spain

Rich and Stephen in courtyard, LLeida, Spain. (photo by Ben Sussman)

above: Rich and Stephen on high speed train in Spain. (photo by Ben Sussman)

below: Stephen and Rich with guest Spanish musicians Hector Rodrigo Ferrus and Jordi Gallen at the Musique Disperses Festival, Lleida, Spain. (photo by Ben Sussman)

lullaby

lullaby, lullaby, lullaby

we do sing it, we do breathe it, we do live in it

lullaby, butterfly, lullafy, butterby, flutterby, fly lullaby

we do sing it, we do breathe it, we do live in it

lullaby, lullaby, lullaby

above: Jen in The Enchanted Forest.

lullaby (cont.)

above: John Savage—flute

Horn in F

above: Jen Harrison—horn

above: Stephen with his first guitar. His life and the life of The Tree People wait to unfold.

let me count the ways

(With a deep bow to Elizabeth Barrett Browning)

Oh Tree People how do I love thee? Let me count the ways!

I love thee to the depth and breadth and height Rich's deep and
    sonorous bass can reach

I love thee to the beckoning sonic level of the intricate cigar boxes
    resting beside Stephen's hips

I love thee freely, as women strive for connection

I love thee purely, as the delight in Maeve's smile when her lips
    touch the kazoo

I love thee with passionate desire as I wait to hear Stephen's lyrics
    lilt through Dead Aunt Thelma's

I love thee with a love as deep as Ron's silent laughter when his
    octapad resonates his magnificent beats

I love thee with the measured breath and precision of John's
    mighty saxophone,

And if the stars continue to align,

I shall love thee, my dearest Tree People,

Until the infinite spiral of Jen's horn guides me into the next dimension

—Julie Keefe, April 22, 2022

the land of

the return of the tree people

the tree people

meet the artists

Stephen Cohen, a.k.a. 3 Hand Stephen, is a performing, recording and visual artist, writer, composer and singer/songwriter, and a founding and forever member of The Tree People band. He has performed in concerts and at festivals across the United States and in Belgium and Spain. His visual art has been featured at galleries, art fairs and festivals in Oregon and California. *Baggy Red Pants and Other Stories*, Stephen's book of short stories, lyrics, poems and visual art, was published by Wake-Robin Press in 2021.

Hailing from a small logging town on the Columbia River, Rich Hinrichsen, a.k.a. Tango Cowboy, is a double bassist, singer, composer, and arranger, and a member of The Tree People since 2007. A highlight of his musical career was traveling with The Tree People to Spain to play at a festival in Lleida. His love for melody, off-beat rhythms, colorful harmony, and poetry drew him to The Tree People. He published a book of cowboy songs *Sing Along Cowboy!* and a book for singers *Sing the Cowboy Way* and he arranged dozens of tangos for a small orchestra.

Julie Keefe is an artist with 25+ years' experience working primarily in documentary and community-based art. Her work includes installations and collaborations with a variety of institutions, health care organizations, artists, children and communities, including the *Ask the Question Project*, a multi-layered project that worked with suicide attempt survivors in the NW to tell their stories with the goal of saving lives and breaking stigma, *Hello Neighbor*, a state-wide public art project, in collaboration with Caldera's youth program, employing a social practice model in neighborhoods affected by change, and using interviews and photographs to introduce children to their neighbors and ultimately neighbors to each other by displaying largescale photographic portraits.

From 2013 to 2017 she served as Portland's inaugural Creative Laureate, a position that uses the Office of the Mayor, and the Laureate role, as a platform to advocate for the arts, arts education, equity, creative industries and practice and Portland's overall cultural health.

wake
robin

For this and other titles available from Wake-Robin Press, please visit:
www.wakerobinpress.com

Also available through Ingram, Amazon.com, Bookshop.org, Barnesandnoble.com,
Powells.com and by special order through your local bookstore.

Lightning Source UK Ltd.
Milton Keynes UK
UKHW050026210522
403330UK00009B/71